Homework!

by
Evelyn Neufeld

Cuisenaire Company of America, Inc.
New Rochelle, New York

For Helen Elizabeth Neufeld

Cuisenaire Company of America, Inc.
Copyright 1987 by Cuisenaire Company of America, Inc.
12 Church Street, Box D, New Rochelle, New York 10802

ISBN 0-914040-56-1

INTRODUCTION

Young children, even before they enter school, are counters. They point at things and use traditional counting words, although not always in the conventional sequence at first. It is not uncommon, for example, to hear a two-year-old child counting, "One, two, three, ten, nine". This book of activities attempts to capitalize upon this apparently natural trait in young children. Almost every page begins with some sort of counting activity before going on to challenge the child with the more difficult task of observing the relationships involved in other components of a good mathematics program such as measurement, geometry, estimation, logic, classification (observing likenesses), and seriation (ordering).

Most learning theorists agree that young children are at a developmental level where cognitive growth can best be enhanced by an emphasis on physically active work. Work done at home is particularly suited to this mode of working. While there is counting, classifying, seriating, measuring, estimating, problem solving, and geometry, the activities in this book are always first done by moving around the home or neighborhood and only later more formally. Always the main purpose is to engage the student's mind.

Preschool and early elementary school-aged students tend to be curious, social, constantly in motion, and judging things by their appearances rather than by any kind of logical evaluation. Many of them return from school before their parents get home. Some of them have spent most of their school time on paper and pencil or workbook activities. This book is intended to provide an active, exploring, thoughtful, and manipulative approach to homework that complements regular school work. The belief is that children cannot learn important concepts from being told them. They must, instead, construct knowledge for themselves through active involvement with the objects and people in their environments. Active, interactive, and thoughtful homework promotes awareness of people and objects in the home, school and neighborhood. It forms the foundation for later more abstract work.

Ideally, teachers and/or parents should select pages from the book which seem appropriate to the developmental level of the child, the particular occasion (such as a holiday, vacation trip or birthday), and/or the environment in which the child lives or visits. A good rule to follow is that any topic that will be taught in a more symbolic form (such as the textbook) two years hence, should now be experienced by the student in an active way method using manipulative materials.

Worthwhile active, mind-engaging work for young children has the following characteristics:

1. It is physically and mentally active. Counting things, measuring things and the passing of time, global comparisons of things or groups of things, handling things, turning things, flipping things over, sliding things, making or noticing patterns of things, guessing or estimating outcomes, sorting things and counting them, ordering things and counting them, recording and discussing findings, and facing many questions beginning with "How many" and "How much" but moving toward questions of "How many kinds of ...?", "How did you figure that out?", "How do you know?", "How long do you think it will take to ...?", "How far do you think ...?", "Was your guess close?", "Which has the most (or least)?" and questions about value judgments such as "Which is your best friend's favorite ...?"

2. It is social. Children at the pre-operational (pre-logical) level of thought, learn and develop from interactions with friends and family members. Thinking work should involve discussions with others whenever possible. Active homework promotes family interactions when parents and/or other family members become directly involved with the physical experiences, the various discussions, and the final outcomes. While the child should do all of the work of counting, measuring, and answering questions, other family members will probably have to do the recording at first (in the case of the preschool/kindergarten child) and engage in the conflict resolution that will arise from relatively open-ended assignments that will be carried out in a variety of settings.

3. It is developmental. The less experience the child has (often age-related; however, older children have sometimes missed out on critical basic experiences necessary for later more complex concepts and younger children have sometimes experienced a particularly rich basic education at home or at school), the more the emphasis should be on manipulating objects, counting them, sorting them, and the less the emphasis should be on recording findings. It should move the child from concrete, physical activities to more abstract, symbolic work. After children have had adequate experience simply handling objects in sorting and counting, they should be encouraged to record their findings. Recordings may take the form of drawing pictures, coloring spaces, or writing numerals to represent the number of things counted or the measurements taken.

4. It is interesting. Even though children often must do things they would prefer to avoid, it is a fact that when their interest is engaged, their energy level increases and they will be more likely to get started on the homework on their own, not to resist it when it is assigned, and to continue doing it beyond what the actual assignment requires. When mind-engaging work is active, it can be done before school, after school, in the evenings, on holidays, on vacation, and on weekends. It will not rob children of needed movement and exercise.

5. It is interdisciplinary. Thoughtful, active work is basic to and promotes not only mathematics but vocabulary development, language acquisition, and exposure to concepts usually associated with other school topics such as science, music, history, geography, art, literature, social studies and physical education.

6. It is easily adapted to the experiences, interests, and living environments of individual children.

7. It exposes children to relatively difficult ideas before they have the ability to fully understand them. This early experience provides the foundation for the eventual understanding which is always the goal.

8. It provides the foundational experience for the textbook material children do at school. Ideally, whatever the child will do more formally in a textbook or workbook one or two years from now, should at this time be introduced in a physically active, way usually using manipulative materials and always in a way that the child's mind is engaged through good questions or assignments that promote questions in the child's mind. There is good reason to believe that without these active foundations, children may be handicapped in later mathematics when memorizing and rote learning can no longer support the non-thinking student.

NOTE TO TEACHERS AND/OR PARENTS

Making Assignments

Children with the least experience in counting and comparing numbers of things and the least experience with working with measuring things or noticing characteristics about things or people should do the section labeled *Pre-Stage Activities*. If these children have not yet been to school or for some other reason cannot yet write numerals, a family member, teacher, or aide may accompany the child and write the responses as things are counted and discussed.

Children with some experience should do the section labeled *Transitional Stage Activities*. They will do their own recording of their responses but will still discuss with family members or children at school or in the neighborhood their results. It is important that these children not be corrected about inadequate responses (from the adult perspective) because they are moving from a stage where they could not think logically at all to a stage where they will be able to think logically. In the transition stage they tend to vacillate between the two stages. It is important that they do not feel that they cannot do mathematics when, in fact, they can do alot, but it is not always at first reasonable and sometimes the numerals are reversed and most of the time the numerals are written large and "messy". The suggestion here is that corrections should not be made; instead, good questions should be asked that might direct the child toward grasping the inconsistency in the response or the direction of numerals on the page. Where reversed numerals are involved, usually the less said the earlier the problem disappears.

Children who have completed the earlier experiences in this book or who have had similar experiences with other programs will be more challenged by the activities in the section labeled *Logical Stage Activities*. It is still of the utmost importance for these children to have their assignments presented in such a way that they will be handling objects, interacting with people, making estimates ahead of time, thinking about how close their estimates were to the actual result, and working with pictures of things. All children need to work with things and be otherwise physically and mentally active, if they are to develop the increasing ability to think abstractly. More experienced students should not solve problems with objects if they can do them without objects. Instead, those things they can solve without objects should be done so, but there should always be activities in their programs that are too difficult for them to do without blocks or other materials they can handle. At this stage, discussion should be particularly encouraged in order for students to continually encounter conflicting answers and viewpoints.

It is in the student's resolution of the various ways of thinking that the student constructs true knowledge. It is important to note that any page in the book is appropriate for any child who shows a special interest in it, regardless of age or grade level. In some cases, for example, part of a page that is generally too difficult for a less experienced child will be entirely appropriate for a particular child. Later (days, weeks or months) that child will complete those parts of the page that were meaningless at the earlier time. Teachers and parents are urged to watch for signs of boredom or extreme frustration (a little frustration is often an indication of an exactly appropriate task) and use these signs as indications of mis-assigned work. Preconceived notions of what a child can or cannot do, however, should be examined. They are often found not to be useful since children almost always surprise adults, sometimes in the direction of being able to do something that seems to be too difficult, and other times, by not being able to do something that traditionally teachers and/or textbook authors assumed that they would be capable of doing or should be taught to do, even if it proved to be an arduous task on the part of the teacher. The suggestion is to assign pages according to students' prior experience but sometimes assign pages that fall in one of the other categories, especially if a particular child begs to do them.

Above all, whether assignments are made by the teacher or the parents, whether work is done independently or with an entire family or class, keep it somewhat light-hearted. Math is really thought-provoking, active, challenging and fun!

Time Considerations

In general, the less experienced the child the shorter the length of time should be, that homework would be expected to be done. Since the assignments suggested in this book are designed to engage children physically and mentally, children sometimes are willing to spend a great deal of time. It is better, however, to stop the assignment before children get tired because they will then be more likely to want to go back to it at another time. Some of the tasks involve family members or friends and are quite time consuming. They can go on for hours, days, or even weeks. Each assignment should be given the amount of time that will result in the greatest amount of cognitive or social development for the child without undue stress or fatigue.

Collection of Assignments

Parents: Parents or others working with children at home are encouraged to discuss each item on an assignment page. Instead of correcting or marking things "right" or "wrong", ask the child how the answer was found. In rehearsing the method used to find the answer, the child often finds the need to correct the inaccurate responses since new data has been found. Pages that were of special interest can be repeated many times.

Teachers: When students return the assignments, their results can be used to make class graphs. They can take the form of bar graphs (answering, for example, how many pieces of mail were received by the families represented)or picture graphs of every kind. It is particularly important not to make judgments about the accuracy of the data received. It would be damaging not to believe a child's data if it should somehow be true. If it is not true, it can be attributed to an earlier developmental level. Always proceed with the graphing on the basis that the information is as accurate as the child is able to give at this time.

PRE-STAGE ACTIVITIES

For children who are quite new to homework assignments and with little experience in counting and thinking about the numbers of things and people, the sizes and shapes of things, the likenesses and differences between things and generally the way things and groups of things and people are related.

HOW MANY DOORS?

Guess how many doors you think you will find in your home._____

Count the doors in your home.

Outside doors_____

Inside doors_____

Other kinds of doors:

Cupboard doors_____

Closet doors_____

Patio doors_____

Refrigerator doors_____

Furniture doors_____

Medicine cabinet doors_____

Garage doors_____

_____ _____

_____ _____

How many doors altogether in your home?_____

Was your guess close?_____

HOW MANY WINDOWS?

Guess how many windows are in your home._____

Count the windows in your home. List them by rooms.

ROOM	NUMBER OF WINDOWS	NUMBER OF PANES
Your room	_____	_____
Your parent's bedroom	_____	_____
Your sister's bedroom	_____	_____
The living room	_____	_____
The dining room	_____	_____
The kitchen	_____	_____
The bathroom	_____	_____
The family room	_____	_____
The garage	_____	_____
The attic	_____	_____
_____	_____	_____

Which room has the most windows?_____

Which room has the most panes?_____

HOW MANY CEREAL BOXES?

Guess how many cereal boxes are in your home._____

Count the cereal boxes in your home.

NAME	NUMBER OF BOXES	NAME	NUMBER OF BOXES

How many different kinds of cereal did you count?_____

How many boxes of cereal did you count?_____

Which is your favorite?_____

Which is your best friend's favorite?_____

How many different kinds of cereal do you think there are in the market?_____

Next time you go shopping with your dad or mom, count the different kinds of cereals in the market.

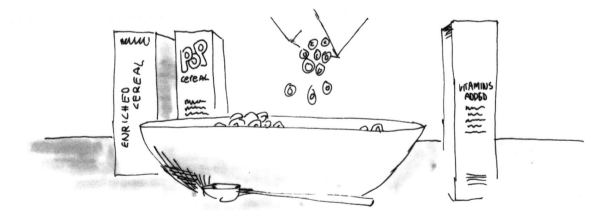

HOW MANY EYES?

Guess how many eyes are in your home. _____

Count the eyes in your home.

Human eyes_____

Pet eyes_____

Toy eyes_____

Total number of eyes_____

Guess how many pairs of eyes there are in your home. _____

Count the pairs of eyes in your home.

Human pairs of eyes_____

Pet pairs of eyes_____

Toy pairs of eyes_____

Total number of pairs of eyes _____

Are there more eyes or more pairs of eyes?_____

Find some other kinds of eyes:

Bull's eye

Eye of a needle

Potato eyes

_____

_____

_____

HOW MANY NOSES?

Guess how many noses you think you will find in your home._____

Count the noses in your home.

Human noses _____

Pet noses _____

Toy noses _____

How many noses altogether?_____

(Did you remember to count your own nose?)

Are there more noses or eyes in your home?_____

Are there more noses or people in your home?_____

Each human nose has two openings called nostrils.

How many nostrils are there in your home?_____

Guess how many noses and eyes there are in your home._____

Human noses and eyes _____

Pet noses and eyes _____

Toy noses and eyes _____

How many noses and eyes altogether?_____

HOW MANY TOES?

Guess how many toes you think you will find in your home._____

Count the toes in your home.

	RIGHT FOOT	LEFT FOOT
Parents' toes	_____	_____
Brothers' toes	_____	_____
Sisters' toes	_____	_____
Other toes	_____	_____
Your toes	_____	_____

Total number of right foot toes _____

Total number of left foot toes _____

How many toes altogether?_____

Without counting, how many fingers do you think there are in your home?_____

Are there more fingers than toes?_____

Are there more toes than fingers?_____

Are there the same number of toes and fingers?_____

How many little fingers are there?_____

How many thumbs are there?_____

How many big toes are there?_____

HOW MANY SHOES?

Guess how many shoes you think you will find in your home. _____

Count the shoes in your home.

Your shoes _____

Your parents' shoes _____

Your brothers' shoes _____

Your sisters' shoes _____

Other shoes _____

Total number of shoes? _____

How many pairs of shoes are in your home? _____

Are there more shoes or more pairs of shoes? _____

How many shoes do not have a matching one? _____

How many shoes are in your closet? _____

Arrange your shoes in pairs. How many pairs? _____

Are there more shoes or more feet in your home? _____

THINGS TO COUNT IN YOUR HOME

How many people are in your home?_____

How many rooms in your home?_____

How many bedrooms?_____

How many bathrooms?_____

How many kitchens?_____

How many beds?_____

How many television sets?_____

How many tables?_____

How many radios?_____

How many clocks?_____

How many watches?_____

How many automobiles?_____

How many refrigerators?_____

How many chairs?_____

How many pets?_____

Are there more beds or bedrooms in your home?_____

Are there more people or pets in your home?_____

COUNTING AT HOME

How many doors? _____

How many windows? _____

How many faucets? _____

How many mirrors? _____

How many closets? _____

How many lamps? _____

How many chimneys? _____

How many fireplaces? _____

How many books? _____

How many sofas? _____

How many giants? _____

How many desks? _____

How many dolls? _____

How many telephones? _____

How many pianos? _____

Are there more lamps or more mirrors? _____

Are there more books or more giants? _____

ABOUT SHOES

Count your shoes.

How many shoes?_____

How many pairs of shoes?_____

What colors are your shoes?_____

How many more shoes are there than pairs of shoes?_____

How many shoes does your dad or your mom have?_____

How many pairs of shoes does he/she have?_____

Who in your family has the most shoes?_____

Who has the most pairs of shoes?_____

Who has the biggest shoes?_____

Who has the smallest shoes?_____

Draw a picture of your favorite pair of shoes_____

MAKING PILES OF THINGS

1. Find some toys or other things that come in different colors and sizes.

2. Find a very big piece of paper or cardboard and draw a line down the middle or lay a piece of string down the middle.

3. Put all of the big things on the left side of the paper and all of the little things on the right side of the paper.

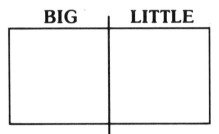

BIG | **LITTLE**

4. Take everything off of the paper and now put all of the red things on the left side of the paper and all of the blue things on the right side of the paper. Things that are not red or blue have no place on the paper.

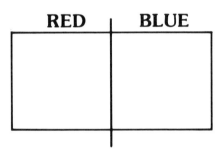

RED | **BLUE**

5. Take everything off of the paper and now put all of the yellow things on the left side of the paper and all of the orange things on the right. What happened to the blue and

red things?_____

_____

_____

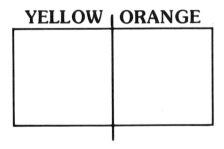

YELLOW | **ORANGE**

This is the LEFT side of the page.

This is the RIGHT side of the page.

MAKING A GRAPH

1. Find some toys or other things that come in different colors and sizes.

2. Find a very big piece of paper and draw some lines from top to bottom and side to side. Make it like the picture on this page.

3. Place as many objects as possible in the matching spaces on your graph.

	RED	YELLOW	BLUE
BIG	SOMETHING BIG & RED HERE		
MIDDLE SIZE			
LITTLE			SOMETHING LITTLE AND BLUE HERE

Could you find a place for purple things?   Yes   No

Could you find a place for red things?   Yes   No

Could you find a place for orange things?   Yes   No

Could you find a place for little things?   Yes   No

Could you find a place for round things?   Yes   No

Could you find a place for things made of plastic?   Yes   No

THINKING ABOUT COLOR, SHAPE, AND SIZE

What kind of an object can you find to go in the space below? _____

Draw its picture in the space.

RED

LITTLE

What kind of an object can you find to go in the space below? _____

Draw its picture in the space.

YELLOW

ROUND

TRANSITIONAL STAGE ACTIVITIES

For students who are able to count easily and quite accurately, who have some experience with writing numerals on their own, who can work with objects or pictures of objects, and who can begin to think about some relationships between objects, groups of objects, number of things, classes of things, and ordered arrangements of things as well as being able to begin to combine numbers of things, to estimate with some accuracy, and to work with some independence even when interacting with others at home or at school.

ALL ABOUT THE MAIL

Count the pieces of mail that are delivered to your house for two days.

DAY 1

How many pieces of mail? _____

How many stamps? _____

How much money was spent on stamps? _____

DAY 2

How many pieces of mail? _____

How many stamps? _____

How much money was spent on stamps? _____

How many pieces of mail altogether in two days? _____

How many pieces of junk mail altogether? _____

How many stamps altogether? _____

How much money was spent on stamps altogether? _____

What is your zip code? ____ ____ ____ ____ ____

What is your grandparents' zip code? ____ ____ ____ ____ ____

ABOUT TRANSPORTATION

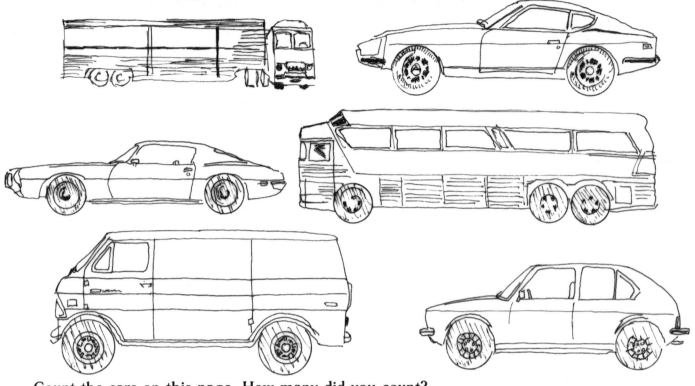

Count the cars on this page. How many did you count?_____

How many vans are there?_____

How many trucks are there?_____

How many buses are there?_____

How many vehicles are there altogether?_____

Circle the one that looks most like the vehicle your family drives.

Which vehicle looks most like the one your best friend's family drives? Color it blue.

Which vehicle looks most like the one your teacher drives? Color it orange.

How many tires can you count?_____

How many tires does each vehicle have?_____

How many vehicles are there altogether?_____

How many tires are there altogether?_____

TOO MANY TO COUNT

When we want to know about how many there are but there are too many to count, we estimate. Estimating is a little like guessing but it takes a little more thinking.

Go shopping with your dad or mom.

Estimate the number of cereal boxes on the shelves._____

Estimate the number of kernels of popcorn in a full jar._____

Estimate the amount of money in coins there is in your home?_____

If possible, count the coins. Were you close?_____

Estimate the number of books in your home._____

Estimate the number of beans in a bag of beans._____

Estimate the number of marshmallows in a bag of marshmallows._____

Estimate the number of blocks from your home to school._____

Count the number of blocks from your home to school._____

Were you close in your estimation?_____

Estimate the number of dishes in your home._____

©1987 Cuisenaire Company of America, Inc.

name

CELEBRATING A BIRTHDAY

**Fill in the name of the person who is having a birthday today.
Draw enough candles.**

How many cakes?_____

How many candles?_____

How many words?_____

How many letters?_____

How many letters in the birthday person's name?_____

Are there more candles or more letters on the cake?_____

Are there more candles, the same number
of candles, or fewer candles than there were last birthday?_____

LETTERS IN A WORD

How many letters are there?_____

Which is the largest letter?_____

Next largest?_____

Next largest?_____

Smallest?_____

Cover all of the letters except the E.

How many letters are smaller than the E?_____

How many letters are larger than the E?_____

Uncover all the letters and check.

Cover all the letters except the B.

How many letters are larger than the B?_____

How many letters are smaller?_____

Uncover all the letters and check.

Print the word "green" the same way and answer the same questions.

ABOUT CARS

How many wheels are usually outside of a car?_____

How many wheels are usually inside?_____

How many tires are usually outside of a car?_____

How many tires are usually inside?_____

Find the diameter (the distance across) of the tires on your family car._____

Find the circumference (the distance around) of the tires on your family car._____

How many windows does your family car have?_____

Which is larger, the front windshield or the rear window?_____

How many mirrors does your family car have?_____

How long is your car?_____ How wide?_____

How many people can ride in your car?_____

How many miles has your car been driven?_____

What is the speed limit on the street in front of your house?_____

What is the speed limit on the street in front of your school?_____

Draw a picture of a family car in the year 2000.

LOOKING AT A WORD

How many letters are there?_____

Which is the largest letter?_____

Next largest?_____

Next largest?_____

Smallest?_____

Cover all of the letters except the E.

How many letters are smaller than the E?_____

How many letters are larger than the E?_____

Cover all the letters except the O.

How many letters are larger than the O?_____

How many letters are smaller?_____

Which three letters are left of the middle?_____

Which three letters are right of the middle?_____

Which is the largest letter left of the middle?_____

Which is the smallest letter right of the middle?_____

Homework!

NAMING BIRTHPLACES

1. Fill in the name of the city, the state, and the country of your birth.

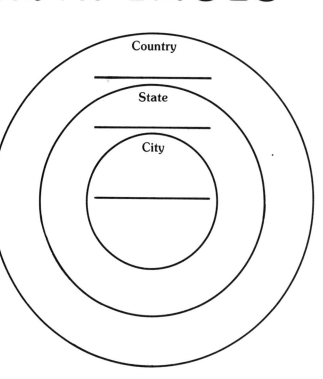

2. Fill in the name of the city, the state, and the country of your father's birth.

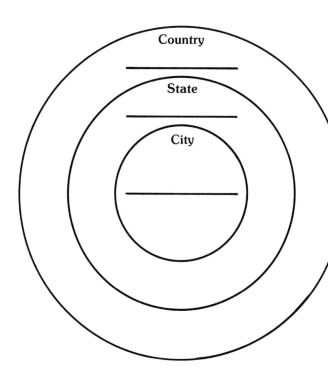

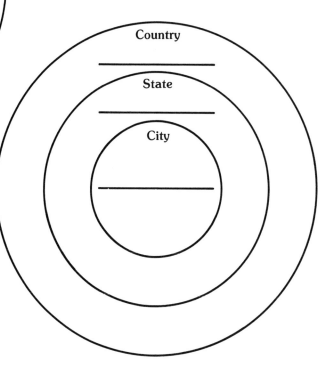

3. Fill in the name of the city, the state, and the country of your mother's birth.

OPEN A CAN OF SOUP

Empty a can of soup into a large pot. Add one can of water. Heat.

What kind of soup do you have?_____

Count the noodles, if you chose Chicken Noodle._____

Name as many of the ingredients as you can recognize.

_____   _____

_____   _____

_____   _____

What color is the soup?_____

About how many tablespoons of soup do you have?_____

How many people will eat the soup?_____

What ingredients can you taste but not see?_____

_____

What ingredient do you think made the soup the color it is?_____

Write the recipe on how you think the soup can be made. (Think about the way it tastes and the way it looks.)

_____

_____

_____

_____

_____

_____

Try making the soup from your recipe.

Is it delicious?_____

A HUNGRY CATERPILLAR

Go to the library and check out *The Very Hungry Caterpillar* by Eric Carle.

Read the book or ask someone to read it to you.

Fill in the missing stages of the development of the caterpillar.

1. egg

2. _____

3. very big caterpillar

4. cocoon

5. a beautiful _____

List all the food that the hungry caterpillar ate.

_____ _____ _____

_____ _____ _____

_____ _____ _____

_____ _____ _____

_____ _____ _____

Put a little mark next to the things that are healthy foods for humans to eat.

A CATERPILLAR'S FOOD

Go to the library and check out *The Very Hungry Caterpillar* by Eric Carle.

Read the book or ask someone to read it to you.

Make a graph of the food the hungry caterpillar ate.

Foods That Are Nutritious

_____

_____

_____

_____

_____

_____

_____

Foods That Are Not Nutritious

_____

_____

_____

_____

_____

_____

_____

CLASSIFYING VEGETABLES

List the canned or fresh vegetables in your home.

_____   _____   _____

_____   _____   _____

_____   _____   _____

Classify according to:

ROOTS	LEAVES	FLOWERS	BULBS	SEEDS	STEMS

Classify according to:

GREEN	YELLOW	RED	BROWN	BLACK	BLUE	OTHER

Examples:

ROOTS	LEAVES	FLOWERS	BULBS	SEEDS	STEMS
carrots	lettuce	broccoli	onions	corn	celery

What is your favorite vegetable?_____

What is your best friend's favorite vegetable?_____

ABOUT DISNEYLAND

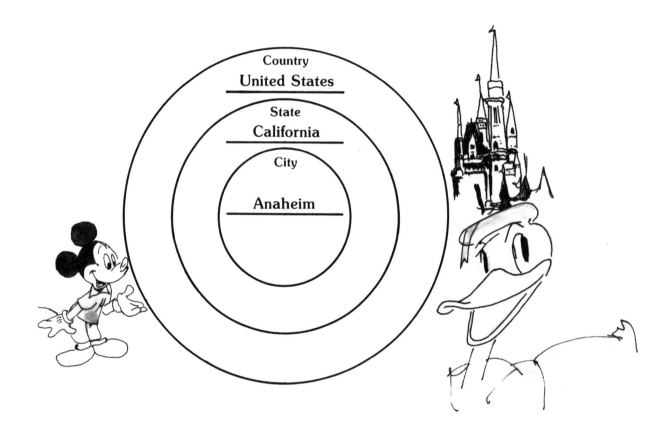

1. Is Disneyland in Anaheim?_____

2. Is Disneyland in California?_____

3. Is Disneyland in the United States?_____

4. Is Disneyland both in California and the United States?_____

5. Is Disneyland in Anaheim, California and in the United States?_____

How many yes answers did you give?_____

How many no answers did you give?_____

Write the address of Mickey Mouse:

			92803
City	State	Country	Zip code

MAKING BIRTHPLACE CIRCLES

Name the city, state and country of your grandparents' birth.

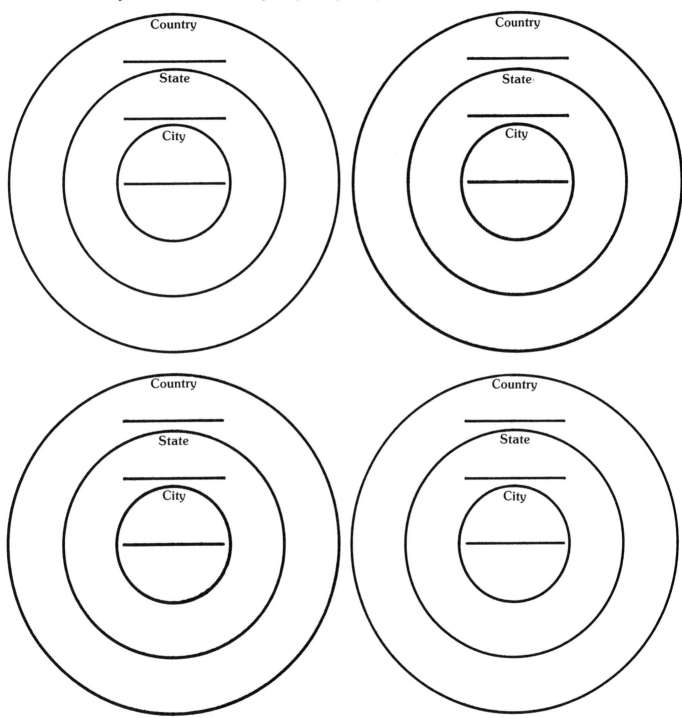

Make other circles to show where your brothers and sisters were born, where your best friends were born, and where the last five presidents were born.

     35

MAKING AN EYE GRAPH

1. Make a list of names of the people who live in your home.

_____   _____   _____

_____   _____   _____

_____   _____   _____

_____   _____   _____

2. Make a list of words that you think would best describe the colors of each person's eyes but the rule is that you cannot use the words blue or brown. Use any other words that remind you of the person's eye color.

_____   _____   _____

_____   _____   _____

_____   _____   _____

_____   _____   _____

_____   _____   _____

3. Now take a close look at the eyes of the people who live with you and make a list of the names of the people with their eye color next to their names. Do not use the same color word for any two people. If you think someone's eyes are the color "rootbeer" then someone else's eyes must be called a different color even though they might be almost the same.

Name of Person   Eye Color

_____   _____

_____   _____

_____   _____

_____   _____

_____   _____

Try the same graph at a family gathering or at school.

LOGICAL STAGE ACTIVITIES

For students who have had more experience counting and comparing, and are able to think about mathematical ideas involving classification, seriation, number, size, movement of objects in space and the relationship involved in these topics as long as they are presented in some pictorial or concrete form.

HOW MANY SWEATERS?

Guess how many sweaters you think you will find in your home. _____

Count the sweaters and their buttons.

	NUMBER	NUMBER OF BUTTONS
Adult sweaters	_____	_____
Children's sweaters	_____	_____

How many sweaters altogether? _____

How many buttons altogether? _____

Are there more sweaters than buttons? _____

Are there more buttons than sweaters? _____

How many people live in your home? _____

Are there more sweaters or people in your home? _____

List the colors of the sweaters in your home.

_____

_____

_____

_____

_____

_____

_____

_____

_____

_____

USING A TELEPHONE BOOK

How many people have your last name?_____

How many people have your best friend's last name?_____

Are there more of your last name or your friend's last name?_____

How many bookstores are in your town?_____
(If you live in a large city, you might want to estimate.)

How many computer stores are in your town?_____

How many pizza restaurants are there in your town?_____

What is the emergency telephone number in your area?_____

What is your area code?_____

What is your grandma's area code?_____

What is your telephone number?_____

What is your grandma's telephone number?_____

What is the telephone number of your favorite store?_____

Name the store_____

On what page is the zip code map?_____

name _____

USING A STATE MAP

Choose a map of your state.

List the cities that begin with the letter S.

_____

_____

_____

_____

_____

How many cities did you find?_____

How many of those cities have you lived in?_____

How many of those cities have you visited?_____

How many people in your family were born in one of those cities?_____

Which city has the most letters altogether?_____

Which city has the fewest letters?_____

Which city beginning with the letter S is nearest the place where you

live?_____

List the cities that begin with the letter F and answer the same questions.

Where were you born? _____ _____ _____
            Country   State   City

LOOKING AT THE UNITED STATES

Use the map of the United States at the bottom of this page.

How many states do you think there are?_____

How many states can you count?_____

Which state looks biggest?_____

Which state looks smallest?_____

Color the map. Use only **4** colors. Try to color touching states different colors.

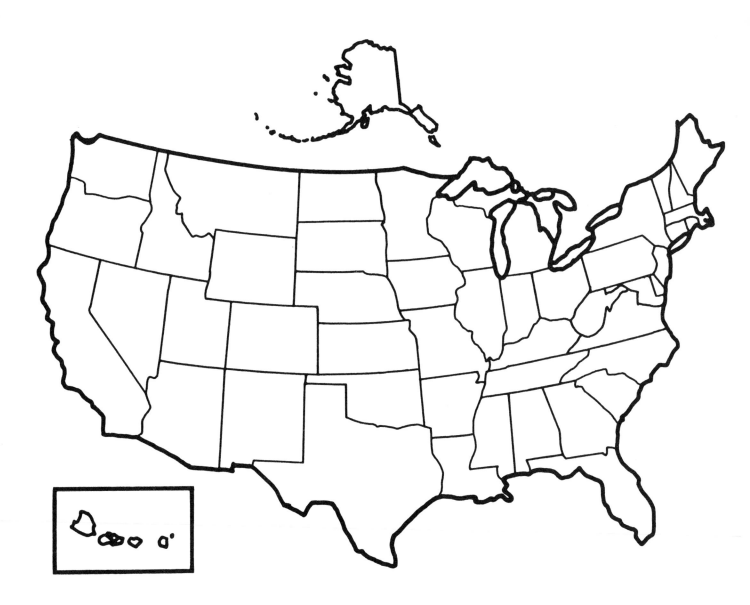

USING A WORLD MAP

Find a map of the world.

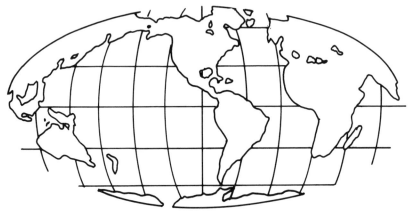

How many countries border the United States?_____

List the countries that border the United States.

_____

_____

Which of the countries that border the United States have you visited? _____

What is the country of your birth?_____

What is the country of your grandfather's birth?_____

List some of the countries that do not border the United States.

_____   _____

_____   _____

_____   _____

How many did you find?_____

How many countries do you think there are in the world?_____

THE GAME OF MONOPOLY

How many stops can be made around the board? _____

How many corners are there?_____

How many jails?_____

How much do you collect when you pass go?_____

Which property costs most to buy?_____

Which property pays the most rent before houses or hotels are built?_____

Have you ever played Monopoly? _____ How many times?_____

Play a game of Monopoly with your family or friends.

What time did you begin?_____

What time did you end?_____

How long did it take?_____

Who won?_____

How much money did the winner have?_____

ABOUT NAMES

How many "t's" are there in the following names?

Your mother's first name_____

Your father's first name_____

Your teacher's last name_____

Your friend's last name_____

Your grandmother's middle name_____

Your grandfather's middle name_____

How many letters are there in the first and last names of the president of the United States?

Write his name and then count.

_____   _____

How many presidents had last names that ended in the letter "n"?_____

Which president had the longest last name?_____

Which president had a last name that has the same first initial as yours?_____

How many presidents have had more than five letters in their last names?_____

Which president had the fewest letters in his last name?_____

What do you think will be the name of the first woman president
of the United States?_____

GOING TO SCHOOL

Estimate the number of houses on your block._____

Count the number of houses on your block._____

How many blocks from your home to school?_____

Estimate how many trees are on your block?_____

Count the number of trees on your block._____

What is the difference between your estimate and the number you counted?_____

How many animals do you see on your way to school in the morning?_____

Circle which kinds: dogs   cats   birds   insects   other

Estimate the number of vehicles you see on your way to school._____

Circle which kinds:

cars	trucks	bicycles	buses	wagons
vans	wheelchairs	motorcycles	tricycles	other
baby strollers	airplanes	trains	rapid transit	

Estimate the height of the tallest building you see on your way to school._____

Is it taller than your school?_____

Is it taller than your house?_____

Estimate the length of the shadow cast
by the tallest tree you see on your way to school._____

THINGS TO COOK

Recipe from *Let's Cook It Right*, Adelle Davis, New American Library, 1970.

Wheat-Germ Muffins

Sift into mixing bowl:
1 cup sifted whole-wheat pastry flour
1 teaspoon salt
3 teaspoons double-acting baking powder
1/4 cup powdered milk

Add and stir only enough to moisten:
1 cup wheat germ
1 cup sweet or sour milk, buttermilk, or yogurt
2 eggs
1/4 cup honey or dark molasses
2 tablespoons vegetable oil
1/2 cup raisins (optional)

Fill paper baking cups or well-greased muffin tins two-thirds full. Bake at 400°F. for 15 to 20 minutes, or until brown. Makes a dozen large muffins.

Write the recipe over so that it will make six (half dozen) large muffins.

_____ cup sifted whole-wheat pastry flour   _____ cup wheat germ

_____ teaspoon salt   _____ cup sweet or sour milk

_____ teaspoons double-acting baking soda   _____ eggs

_____ cup powdered milk   _____ cup honey or dark molasses

_____ tablespoons vegetable oil   _____ cup raisins (optional)

Write the recipe over so that it will make one large muffin.

_____ cup sifted whole-wheat pastry flour   _____ cup wheat germ

_____ teaspoon salt   _____ cup sweet or sour milk

_____ teaspoons double-acting baking soda   _____ eggs

_____ cup powdered milk   _____ cup honey or dark molasses

_____ tablespoons vegetable oil   _____ cup raisins (optional)

Make one large muffin. How long did it have to bake?_____

Which of the following could you add to make the muffin taste better?

walnuts   pecans   chopped dates   ground dried apricots

shredded carrots   finely diced raw apples   stardust

CREATE A RECIPE

Create an original recipe.

A recipe has a name that tells what you will make.

A recipe has a list of ingredients.

A recipe tells how much of each ingredient is needed.

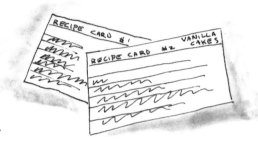

A recipe has directions telling the order in which the ingredients are used, the way in which they should be mixed, the kinds of utensils that are needed, the temperature setting of the oven, the number of minutes needed, and the number of servings.

Try to create a recipe that will be nutritious (no sugar, no preservatives) and that will taste delicious enough to serve your family for dessert.

List some possible ingredients:

_____   _____

_____   _____

_____   _____

_____   _____

Experiment with Jell-o.

1. Make part of the recipe using the amount of water suggested on the box.

2. Make part of the recipe using half cup more of water.

3. Make part of the recipe using one cup more of water.

How much extra water can be added to Jell-o and still have it gel?_____

Which way did you like the Jell-o best, 1, 2, or 3?_____

WAYS TO ESTIMATE

There are many beads on this page. How many ways can you think of to make the job of counting them easier?_____

Estimate the beads._____

Count the beads._____

Some methods are given on page 49.

Were your methods better?_____

COUNTING LARGE NUMBERS OF THINGS

Here are some methods for counting large numbers of things:

1. Guess.

2. Count in groups of ten. Draw a line after every ten things.

3. Color each group of ten a different color.

4. Number the things from 1 to …

5. Count some of the beads. Then estimate how many more there are.

6. Get a friend to help you.

7. Get your mom or dad to help you.

8. Wait until you are older.

Your methods:

9. _____

10. _____

11. _____

12. _____

Place a check (✓) beside those methods you used.

Place an (X) beside the method that worked best for you.

What is the largest number of things you have ever counted?_____

What can you think of that would be impossible to count?_____

Approximately how many strands of hair do you think you have on your head?_____

THINKING ABOUT ADDRESSES

What is your house number and street name? _____

Who lives to the right of your house when you face it? _____

What is the house number and street name of the house to your right? _____

Who lives to the left of your house when you face it? _____

What is the house number and street name of the house to your left? _____

Who lives across the street from you? _____

What is the house number and street name
of the house across the street from you? _____

Do the houses on your side of
the street have house numbers that are odd or even? _____

Notice the house number of your grandparents' home. Is it odd or even? _____

What is your best friend's address? _____

Circle the last digit in the house number. Is it odd or even? _____

Which has the highest house number,
the house to the left of yours or the house to the right? _____

Notice the house numbers of the relatives you visit.

Write the name of the person whose house has the lowest number.

_____   _____
      Name   Number

DRAWING A MAP OF YOUR ROOM

North

West   East

South

Your bed is on the _____ wall? (North, South, West, or East)

What is in the northwest corner of your room?_____

The windows face what direction(s)? _____

What is in the southwest corner of your room?_____

What direction are you facing when you sit up on your bed?_____

When you leave your room do you turn right, left or go straight ahead to go to your

kitchen?_____

COUNTING ON YOUR BIRTHDAY

What is the date of your birth?

_____   _____   _____
The Month   The Day   The Year

Make a list of the children in your family. List the youngest child first and the oldest child last.

NAME   **BIRTHDAY**

_____   _____

_____   _____

_____   _____

_____   _____

How old are you today?_____

How old were you two years ago?_____

How old will you be 23 years from now?_____

How old will you be in the year 2000?_____

How many people are celebrating your birthday with you?_____

What kind of a present would you like?_____

How old was the United States the year you were born?_____

©1987 Cuisenaire Company of America, Inc.

SLICING A BIRTHDAY CAKE

Pretend that this is a real cake and that there are 6 people at your party.

Cut the cake (by drawing vertical and horizontal lines) so that each person may have the same size piece and that no cake is leftover.

How many pieces do you have?_____

How many cuts from top to bottom?_____

How many cuts from left to right?_____

Does your cut up cake look something like this? _____

Across the top there are how many parts?_____

Along the side there are how many parts?_____

How many horizontal rows?_____ How many vertical columns?_____

When there is a cake (or array) that has two rows and three columns,

how many pieces are there?_____   2 x 3 =_____

When there is a cake (or array) that has three rows and two columns,

how many pieces are there?_____   3 x 2 = _____

CUTTING UP A BIRTHDAY CAKE

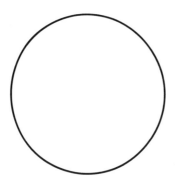

Pretend that this is a real cake and that there are 3 people at your party.

Cut the cake so that each person may have the same size piece and that no cake is leftover.

Are there 3 pieces?_____

Is there any cake leftover?_____

Are the three pieces the same size?_____

If you had some cake left over or the three pieces are not the same size, practice on lots of cakes to see if you can do it. Try to do it by yourself without the help of your teacher, your parents, your brothers and sisters, or your friends.

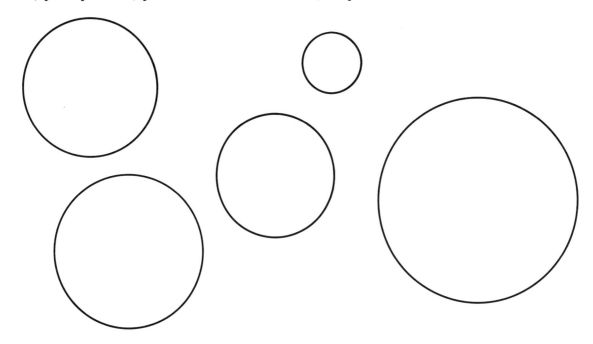

COUNTING ON VALENTINE'S DAY

Count the number of Valentine cards you are giving. _____

Count the number of hearts on the cards you are giving. _____

How many cards are going to friends? _____

How many cards are going to relatives? _____

What is the date of Valentine's Day? _____

_____   _____
           The Month   **The Day**

In what part of the month is Valentine's Day?

Beginning _____

Middle _____

End _____

Draw a picture of your favorite Valentine from a friend.

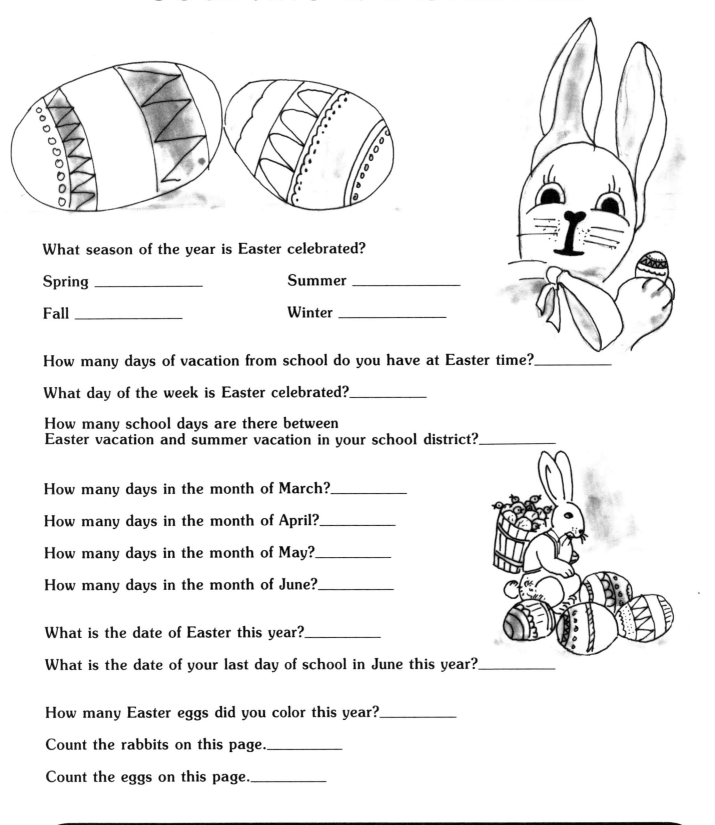
Homework!

COUNTING AT EASTER TIME

What season of the year is Easter celebrated?

Spring _____   Summer _____

Fall _____   Winter _____

How many days of vacation from school do you have at Easter time?_____

What day of the week is Easter celebrated?_____

How many school days are there between
Easter vacation and summer vacation in your school district?_____

How many days in the month of March?_____

How many days in the month of April?_____

How many days in the month of May?_____

How many days in the month of June?_____

What is the date of Easter this year?_____

What is the date of your last day of school in June this year?_____

How many Easter eggs did you color this year?_____

Count the rabbits on this page._____

Count the eggs on this page._____

COUNTING ON A TRAVELING VACATION

You can use a real vacation or invent a pretend vacation.

What date did you begin your vacation?_____ _____ _____
                                         Month   Day   Year

Besides the state you live in, how many states did you visit?_____

Estimate the number of towns and cities you traveled through._____

How many days were you away on your trip?_____

How many hours each day did you travel?_____

How many hours was your longest day of travel?_____

How many hours was your shortest day of travel?_____

How many miles or kilometers did you travel altogether?_____

How many relatives did you visit on this trip?_____

Name three of America's best known parks.

_____   _____   _____

How many different states and provinces did you recognize on license plates?_____

If you could plan a "dream vacation" where would you go?_____

VACATION TIME

You can use a real vacation or invent a pretend vacation.

Use a road map that shows your state.

Find your home city or town on the map and put a mark on it.

Find each city and town on the map as you drive through them. Put marks on each one.

Find the road you are traveling along on the map. Trace it with your finger.

Find the point of your destination on the map. Put a big mark on it. Trace the path from your home to the point of your destination. Each day see how much closer to your destination you are moving on the map.

Name the mountain range you must cross, if any. _____

Name any oceans you see on your trip. _____

Name any rivers you cross. _____

How did you cross the rivers? Bridge _____ Ferry _____ Other _____

ON A RAINY SATURDAY

Read some poetry.

THE RAIN

The rain, they say, is a mouse-gray horse
   That is shod with a silver shoe;
The sound of his hoofs can be heard on
   the roofs
As he gallops the whole night through.
From: Rowena Bastin Bennett,
Around a Toadstool Table, (Follett).

THE RAIN

The rain is raining all around,
   It falls on field and tree,
It rains on the umbrellas here,
   And on the ships at sea.

From: Robert Louis Stevenson,
A Child's Garden of Verses.

What time did the rain begin today?_____

Estimate the time that the rain will end._____

Place several containers outside to catch some of the rain. Use bottles, jars or pans in several sizes.

How much rain was gathered in each container?

Use a measuring cup to see how much rain was gathered.

Bottle_____

Jar_____

Pan_____

Other_____

Read some nonsense stories such as *The Cat and the Parrot.*
Read these stories: *The Story of the Three Bears* (L. Leslie Brooke); *The Story of the Three Little Pigs* (L. Leslie Brooke); *Millions of Cats* (Wanda Gag); *The 500 Hats of Bartholomew Cubbins* (Dr. Seuss); *Homer Price,* especially the "Doughnut" chapter, (Robert McCloskey).

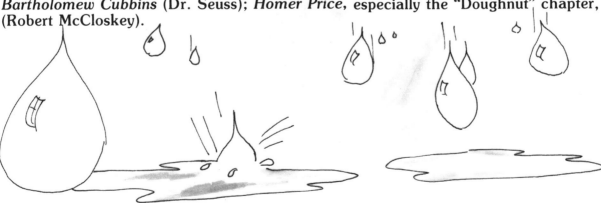

HALLOWEEN NIGHT

What is the date of Halloween? Circle the month, date, day of week.

MONTHS	DATES	DAY OF THE WEEK
January	1 2 3 4 5 6 7	Sunday
February	8 9 10 11 12 13 14	Monday
March	15 16 17 18 19 20 21	Tuesday
April	22 23 24 25 26 27 28	Wednesday
May	29 30 31	Thursday
June		Friday
July	The year is _ _ _ _	Saturday
August		
September		
October		
November		
December		

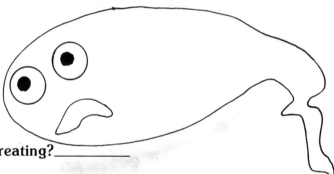

Did you go trick-or-treating?_____

How many items did you collect?_____

What kinds of things did you collect? Circle all the kinds you collected.

Candy   Fruit   Toys   Money   Other

What time did you begin? _____

What time did you end? _____

How long were you trick-or-treating?_____

AT THANKSGIVING TIME

What is the date of Thanksgiving Day this year?

_____   _____   _____
The Month   The Day   The Year

How many days of vacation (including Saturday and Sunday) will you have?_____

What day of the week is Thanksgiving Day? Circle one.

Sunday

Monday

Tuesday

Wednesday

Thursday

Friday

Saturday

How many family members will be together for Thanksgiving dinner?_____

Make a list of all of your relatives. Begin with your own family.

_____   _____   _____

_____   _____   _____

_____   _____   _____

How many things are you thankful for? List them.

_____

_____

_____

COUNTING AT HANUKKAH

The date of Hanukkah this year is _____.

Circle the Jewish month of Hanukkah.

1. Tishri
2. Chesvan
3. Kislev
4. Tebet
5. Sebat
6. Adar
7. Nisan
8. Iyar
9. Sivan
10. Tannuz
11. Av
12. Elul

The Hebrew year is 57__ __

In what year will the next Hanukkah be celebrated?

_____   _____
Modern   Hebrew

How many days is Hanukkah celebrated?_____

How many candles are lit each day?_____

How many candles are lit altogether?_____

How many sides of the dreidel have letters?_____

How many gifts did you receive?_____ How much money?_____

Draw a picture of the menorah on the last day of Hanukkah.

Are there more branches for candles or more Hanukkah days?_____

COUNTING AT CHRISTMAS

How many days until Christmas?_____

What is the date of Christmas?_____

_____   _____
        The Month   The Day

How many Christmas ornaments are on your tree at school?_____

How many Christmas ornaments are on your tree at home?_____

Estimate the number of Christmas trees in the lot where you bought your tree._____

Estimate the number of toys in the toy department of your favorite store._____

How many relatives will have Christmas dinner with you?_____

How many Christmas cards has your family received?_____

How many verses does the Christmas carol "Silent Night" have?_____

How many reindeer does Santa Claus have?_____

Name as many as you can.

_____ _____ _____

_____ _____ _____

_____ _____ _____

What is your favorite Christmas carol?_____

What is your favorite Christmas story?_____

A FAMILY GATHERING

How many great grandparents?_____

How many grandparents?_____

How many uncles?_____ How many aunts?_____

Uncle_____ Aunt_____

Uncle_____ Aunt_____

Uncle_____ Aunt_____

How many cousins?_____
List them from the oldest to the youngest.

_____ _____ _____

_____ _____ _____

_____ _____ _____

How many second cousins?_____
List them from the oldest to the youngest.

_____ _____ _____

Do you have sisters and/or brothers?_____

If you do, name the sister or brother just older than you._____

Name the sister or brother just younger than you._____

If you are a twin, name the sister or brother that is the same age as you are. _____

How old are you? _____ How old is your twin?_____

What is the greatest distance that any
relative traveled to come to the family gathering?_____